Star Chasing

Thomas R. Thomas

Los Nietos Press
Downey California 2019

Published in the United States by
Los Nietos Press
Downey, CA 90240
www.LosNietosPress.com
LosNietosPress@gmail.com

Cover image: da-kuk, istockphoto.com
Author Photo: Alan Passman

First Edition
ISBN-13: 978-0-9984036-7-0

for Michelle

Table of Contents

Star Chasing

I

(Intimate)

ventilator dreams

her child lies
still
on the bed

the ventilator
sits
at her side

slowly pumping
her lungs
her chest rises

in quiet rhythm
mother
sits by her side

hoping the
Doctors
are wrong

God
will send
a miracle

A Love Poem

a love poem
needs to fester

like when you're
twelve riding
your stingray
barefoot and you
scraped the top
of your foot
on the asphalt

and you didn't
take care of it
because you're
twelve and
the grit and
the dirt and
the puss and
the pain totally
gets to you

and you can't
help it because
the pain is so
great that
you finally
have to put
the words down

but you can't
say I love you
I want to live
with you forever

the words have to
be like when you
are so frustrated
that you pound
your fists on the
asphalt and your
knuckles are all
bloody and like
the time your
brother tackled
you in the end zone
which is your asphalt
driveway and your
glasses get a gash
on the lens and
your jeans are ripped
in the knees and
are soaked with
blood or the
time that guy cheated
in the fight and
kicked you in
the balls

those words have to
feel like the pain
and betrayal and
anguish and

that is how to
write a love poem

the ripe avocado

should be firm
with a little give

somewhat like
raising a child

the child could
also use a hug

the avocado
doesn't care

Broken Plate

He watches as
the plate explodes
on the floor.

Afraid to move,
he stands in
his bare feet

with the shattered
shards of plate
covering his feet.

Lifting his feet,
careful where
he steps,

the tiny slivers
stabbing him
at each step

as he stares
at the glass
glistening from

the kitchen light
as he sweeps it up
in the dust pan.

And how does he tell
his wife her special
crystal plate is history?

I am the earth

solid unpretentious

You are the Stars
silent eternal

I long to
be with you

Yet don't know

I already am

we were skinny then

and beautiful

yet

we didn't
know it

longing
for love

we were
golden

a flower
bursting from
the bud

yet

Night Dreams

Reach over to touch
tentative always tentative

a hand pulls from the dark
tugging at the back of my head
to feel your soft warm
nipple in my mouth

the girl you marry

is clustered with

her family
her history
the boys she knew

and not just the
girl you sat with
on the porch that night

as you weaved
your dreams

like your fingers

interlaced

she

time has turned
off the flow
of blood

she

wonders if

time has taken
away her
femininity

he

gently touches
her shoulder
as he passes

Jupiter Loves the Moon

he is sitting
above the moon's
left shoulder

peering over

winking at me

I cannot
reach you

II

(Memories)

cut

let me cut you
so you bleed
the blood that
burns my veins

black and cold

growing slow

then

sudden in
white hot fury

the blood
like tar
smothered in
your upturned palms

impossible to remove

live with it
as it seeps
into your skin

live with
the memory
of your eyes
turned away

you shun me
in fear

fear of touching
my dark soul

too afraid to
stand by my side

to be known as

friend

Bobby - June 5, 1968

I remember the night
Bobby got shot

I was watching
the election
that night

too young to vote
old enough to know

I knew his son
was the same
age as me

thirteen was
too young to
carry such a weight

he sat in his
room in Malibu
watching TV

with me
watching with him
fifty miles away

Bobby carried our
hope on his shoulders

and our hope
fell to the floor
as the busboy
helpless
held his hand

and I've found
it hard to
trust again

Maple Trees

Two maple trees soared
in my backyard

I would climb them
until I would
sway at the top
feel the wind
in my face

wrap my arms
and legs as
tight as
I could hold

I could see
the Eastland
shopping sign
down the
freeway, and

each house
in the
neighborhood

get lost in
the dream of
almost flying

then slowly
carefully climb
down to the
solid earth

leaving my
spirit soaring

Records

I loved buying
a new album

flipping through
the racks to
discover the
first album by
a favorite band

buying the album
and taking it home

slitting the
cellophane with
my thumbnail

and pulling the
record out of
the cardboard sleeve

I loved the
albums
with lyrics

handwritten
by the artist

I would read the
lyrics as I played
the album for
the first time

the words of the
song would carry
such power

carry me with
the music inside
the song

there is nothing
like hearing a
song for the
first time

as the words
pulled me in
into the
soul of the singer

Our First Turkey

Our first turkey
was 25 pounds.

Those were the
days when
the company
gave you a
turkey for
Thanksgiving.

We had to take
the racks out
of the oven
to make it fit.

Michelle called
her Mom Tuesday,
Wednesday, and
four times
Thanksgiving Day.

But Michelle still
forgot to take the
bag of neck, gizzard,
and gross parts
out before she
cooked it.

And she forgot
to truss up
the legs and
wings so the
bird was still
trying to fly
in the oven.

We had just
moved from
Southern
California,

too soon to
make friends
from work
or church.

We were
alone
with no friends
or family.

the huge poplar
trees next door
had filled
the backyard with
brown, red, and orange.

The leaves were covered
with our first snow.

Our little fifties
table filled
with enough
food for twelve,

enough for days
of leftovers,
enough turkey to
share with our
dog and cats,

our little
Oregon family.

Playground

My jungle gyms
were the studs
in the bare walls
of the tract homes
my Dad built.
I climbed them
like a monkey
and ran across
the floor joists
careful not to
fall through
the gaps.

My sandbox was
the piles of sand
waiting for the
bricklayers.
I built tunnels and
spread the sand thin
unaware of the angry
stares of the bricklayers.

I floated sticks down
the rivers of puddles
between the houses—
my jagged fleet
going off to war.

I jumped from second
floor balconies and
splashed the puddles,
rolling and running off
scurrying to some
shelter hiding from
some enemy cloistered
only in my mind.

It's that moment

the first time
you kiss her

the rush of blood
the slight
intake of air

open your eyes
see her eyes
for the first time
lashes touching

hold your lips
in a breath of hers

touching her
soul to soul

never to repeat
that moment

Raking

the rake
my dance
partner

move to the
rhythm
of flying leaves

as they
gather
in crowds

Star Chasing

I knew
everything
I could find

about the
space program
in the sixties

when I was
a boy reading
all the books

I could get my
hands on dreaming
space dreams

and when I
learned in the
nineties SETI

was listening
to the stars for
signs of life

my computers
crunch the
numbers now

doing my
small part

star chasing

binary

the primary
essence of
computing
is binary

0 1

on off

the light
goes on
then off

a hundred
million
billion
times

as fast
as light
speeds on
a glass wire

My life
is binary

on then off

in the flash
of an eye

I am here
then gone

in a

microsecond

of time

Ten Thousand Hours

they say it takes
ten thousand hours
to master a thing

that's a little
over a year

does that mean
if I've served the time

I've mastered
the thing

and at my age
does it mean
I'm a master of life

yet

I've been kicked
in the ass
fifty times

I think life
has won
so far

so in twenty or
thirty more tries

I might master life

or die trying

Letting Go

He called me
into the office
"I'm sorry,
we can't
keep you
any more."

As I carried
the box
out the door
I wondered
why *he* stayed.

Incompetence
must be an asset.

This is the
third time
in the eighties
I was an
undereducated male.

Then the
nineties and
double nothings
were the years
of the failed
startups—too many to count.

All of us
standing
in a group in the
conference room,
all thinking
of the computers
and furniture
we can take home
for a quarter
of the cost.

Now we are all
contract workers.
There are no strings
to attach us.

They let us go
with a phone call,
"Thank you
for your
services."

The words are
different,
but the song
is the same—

greed comes in
different flavors.

It's as if
the rich were
taking the risk,

but *we* are
the ones standing
outside the door
with *just* a
box in our hands.

The Night

we lived for the night
the years I fell into
the broken boys

wavering on the
brink of adulthood

and I had just
emerged from a
greater darkness

cocooned inside
my head emerging
with black wings

school nights
smoking in
the cemetery

passing joints
around in a
tight circle

tapping our
Marlboro boxes
on our palms to
make them last

sharing my
precious smokes

hoping for a
high to make
it through
the night
the week

on Friday nights
we'd buy a six pack
with the lies we
told our parents

hoping for oblivion

and on summer nights
we'd spend all night
on the top of a hill
climb inside a small pill

imagine I am
climbing eternity
hoping for that
final ecstasy
praying that the
night will never end

the arrow

Never give a boy
in the suburbs
a bow and arrow.

Jeff and I stood
in the backyard.
I shot an arrow
high in the air.

Who would have thought
that the arrow
would come down?

it almost hit David
playing football
in the front yard.

The guilt didn't
come for another
15 or 20 years.

I wonder sometimes,
if my arrow would
have taken him
as a boy,

I would we have missed
him less than when
the helicopter,

lost for twenty hours,

took him—

the arrow finally landing.

I wonder, if the
arrow had struck home
when he was a boy,

I could have avoided
the phone call
from Dad
waking me up
Sunday morning.

"Tom, David's gone."

Eternal Flame

11-22-63

He doesn't know
the flame burns
above his grave.

Burning on into
the eons of time,
to never dim

after Arlington
becomes a memory,
then passes from

existence.

The flame will
burn on the bleak
and barren ground.

The future creatures
that roam the earth
will sniff and wonder
at the flame,

then skitter off,
forgetting this
eternal flame.

cleansing

run the blade
swift on the stone

slice the tips
a cross in each

the palm pools, flows
black on the sleeve

fingers vibrate
shiver the frame

eyes cross, the hand
shimmers in the gaze

plant the palm
in the face

grip the forehead
with the tips

blood, sweet
on the tongue

Close the Door

where do we
go when the
body leaves us

I have an idea

but who has
traveled there
and returned

I'm looking
forward to
knowing

I am waiting

III

(Family)

Papa's Bourbon

bourbon rests
in the mason jar —
small, perfect for jam —
amber aged to perfection
in the cask, bottled at just
the right time

the real thing is
only from Kentucky
the bottle treasured
in the leather case

take a sip, then raise
the jar to Papa
who nods a smile

Father to Son

During the depression
Dad would hunt, trap, and
plow the neighbor's fields.

As the oldest son
he needed to help
pay for the food
for a large family.

He could get
twenty-five cents
from the government
for a crow beak.

Enough crow beaks,
beaver pelts, and
sweat and blood
left on a
neighbor's field,

you can feed the
family for a week.

A boy becomes a
man in short order,

always wondering
why his own son
can't see life
in the same way.

Hobo Stew

Dad and me made
Something we called
Hobo Stew.

Everything but the
ground beef
came out of a
can or jar.

We even got
a little fancy
with marinated
artichoke hearts.

I still use the
artichoke hearts
in my spaghetti sauce.

But I'm just a
cook out of a can,
just like Dad.

Watts

Dad worked from the
mountains to the ocean
from Bel Air to Watts

I went to work with
him for as long
as I can remember

riding in his
pickup on every
freeway in LA

listening to his
stories growing up
in Kansas and
as a Marine
in the Pacific

I remember one
day when I
was eleven
not long after
the Watts Riots
sitting with
an old Black
man on the
sidewalk in Watts

and him
telling me
to call him …

well, he used
that word

I didn't
answer him

I can never
tell if
someone
teases me

I couldn't
tell then

I couldn't
say it then

I can't
say it now

even if he
really wants
me to say it

Humming

Sometimes I envy Dad,
he always worked alone
except when he needed
to lift a beam,
or yell at me through
the floor as I lay on
the dark cold ground
under the joists.

Humming the same hymn
I could never identify.

I work in small cubicles
or tables with two foot
walls crammed like a chicken
with enough room
to eat and drop my eggs—
never enough room to
spread my wings.

I hum and tap my feet.
It's how I think.
Often someone will
tap me in the shoulder
and ask me to stop.
Holding it in is
like a dam holding
back a flood.

One day I won't have
to go into the office.
I'll have the time
to work alone to do
what I want to do.

Dream my dreams
weave my words

and hum to my
hearts content

Birthday

tomorrow is Dad's
birthday
he'd be 94
gone fourteen years

it seems
the anger
burns more
now

though
the love
is never
gone

In which my Puritan ancestor visits me in a waking dream

and another thing, you're just dressed in a t-shirt.

but I'm home alone in my couch.

but it's shameful. God will condemn you,

God doesn't care what I wear at home.

and you should be ashamed

well, you might have something there. I don't have
the body of a thirty-year-old,

of yourself and cover your shame.

and I can't imagine God made this body, and look at
you you're just a skeleton in a Puritan outfit.

Well, I'm dead you know.

that you are, and besides some nights even a t-shirt is
too much clothing, but I can't take it off all because of
you damn Puritans - thank you very much.

You're welcome.

That's one thing you Puritans gave to America.

Shame.

Shame, thank you very much.

You're welcome. What's America?

IV

(Stories)

Promises

don't tell mommy
promise, promise me

she tells me with
every other little
thing she tells me

so full of
promises her
daddy makes
her keep
from mommy

filling so full
she'll break
one day

she sits small

in the grocery aisle
hugs the floor
barely glance
as I pass

the little dreamer
must get away
to her escapes

April celebrates

Libraries, Autism, and
Poetry there is

an equation there somewhere
it will grow on me in time

Waiting

she walks the
magazine racks
slow

her sweatshirt
off her bare
shoulders

flipping the pages
she waits at the front

as her mother pushes
the cart in the
checkout

she pulls the
sweatshirt
over her shoulders

the same sadness
still on her face

She Breaks Free

the light from the
cracks in the door
glows green
—a unique color

this door
is wrong
staring at her
from the middle
of the floor

she stares back
warm in the
comfort of
her blankets

she closes her eyes
shakes her head
opens them quick
as if to sneak
up on the door

it's still there

four lines
glowing green
in the night

still cloaked
in the blanket
she creeps
slowly to
the door

searching for
the handle

she sits
cross-legged
bundled in
the blankets

no handle

with her small
fingers she reaches
in the crack and
pulls - slightly

the door lifts
open on its
own power

leaving her
blanket behind

dressed only in
her tattered PJs
she steps in
turning her
world sideways
in the magic below

Pavlov's Cat

now when
I open
a can

he climbs the
cabinets

hoping

for his small
taste of tuna

hopeless

shuffle stilted walk
you drift through
we invisible you

breasts bounce
in ill fitting
castoff clothes

blank stare
even you can't
stand the smell

sanity gone
stopped being
a woman

too long
to remember
stopped being

human
stopped
being

hapless

the sun is shining
through the blanket
shadows of the
leaves are dancing
in the breeze

he works himself
comfortable
in the slope
brushing the
wood chips away

wrapping the
blanket tight
around his
shoulders

he fingers
the empty
frames of his
old glasses
pulling them
slightly out
of his pocket

watching as the
cars glide by
fuzzy in-flight pass
in the distance

sitting in
his cocoon
world

a small bug
skitters across
his hand

he watches
relishing
the company

stares at the
dark blotches
on his skin
rubs at
the dirt patch

remembers
text books
classrooms
pencils

staff meetings
deans and
sabbaticals

watching as
the feet and
car wheels
pass him by

Celebrity

so the kids
called to me
told me
Hurry

we all ran
down B Street
between the
wash and

the empty
tract that
was waiting
forever for
the new homes

and there
he was
the sheriff
from that show

waiting in
the car
trying to
avoid our gaze

Ode to a $10 Bill

why couldn't
it have
been the 5

that fell on
the floor

First Date

the taste of blood
burning the blade
lingered
on her tongue

she looked down on him
the glint in her eye
pulled up the
corners of her mouth

as if this were love

his eyes stared up
at her unblinking

she turned, leaving
the blade point down
in the asphalt

and under him a
darkness grew

drifting a river
down the white line

V

(Drifting)

Mathew Brady

in his time
the subject
had to be
still

for a few
seconds

people did
not smile

his favorite
subjects

were the
war torn dead
lying quietly

posing for him
where they died

in my dreams

I can run
and not grow tired

making me want to
stay longer in
my dreams

living again
the days of
my youth

when running
was like flying

Remember

Remember, the rope on
his collar shouldn't be
too short or too long
so he could jump
part way over
the fence.

I still leave the
last bite on my
plate for him.

Underwater

If I could
I would
live underwater

dolphin swim
the length
of the pool

pop up
only when
starving for air

at the beach
dive down to the sand
just beyond
the breaking waves

grab a handful
then rest
at the bottom

push up
break the surface
stare up
at the cloudless blue

as the sand
washes slowly
from my open palm

back in the pool
play scuba diver

lost in my
great adventure

then drift
slowly
to the bottom
of the pool

staring at the
surface as the
chlorine makes
my eyes
lightning red

Present Perfect

I'm always getting
my tenses wrong

I keep flitting
to the past
and future

I can't seem
to find
the present

Smart Phone

my smart phone
doesn't know
the word fuck

I swype the
keyboard -
I get duck
Dick (close)
tuck - but

no fuck

I guess it
knows better
than me

cluck – damn

The jelly

(you know it's
 not a fish)
is smarter
than we thought

floating
in my face
in the sea
I've seen
them smile.

homeless haiku

stuck inside my head
it's lonely in here
broken dreams

silent night
shattered stars in my eyes
I remember you

cold wet ground
can't get comfortable
can't ever sleep

Among the Savages

tight stomach
nerves on edge
out of breath
run and hide
palms sweat

I am invisible

Acknowledgements

"Hopeless" and "hapless" first appeared in *Homeless* (Silver Birch Press).

"Promises "and "The Night" first appeared in *Climbing Eternity* (Weekly Weird Monthly).

"In which my Puritan ancestor visits me in a waking dream" first appeared in *Black-Listed Magazine*.

"Eternal Flame" and "Underwater" first appeared in *Cadence Collective*.

"Star Chasing", "binary", "the girl you marry", and "ventilator dreams" first appeared in *East Jasmine Review*.

"First Date" first appeared in *Lummox Press*.

"Pavlov's Cat" first appeared in *RCC MUSE* Magazine.

"the jelly" first appeared in *Whiskey Fish Review*.

About the Author

Thomas R. Thomas was born in Los Angeles, California, and grew up in the San Gabriel Valley east of Los Angeles. Currently he lives in Long Beach, California. He has been writing poems and stories since he was 18. His books include *Scorpio* (Carnival, 2012), *Five Lines* (World Parade Books, 2013), *Climbing Eternity* (Weekly Weird Monthly, 2016), *the art of invisibility* (Dark Heart Press, 2018), and *In Which the World is Turned Upside Down* (Alien Buddha Press, 2018). His poems have appeared in numerous journals and anthologies including *Don't Blame the Ugly Mug, East Jasmine Review, Siver Birch Press Summer Anthology, Cultural Weekly, Pipe Dream, Bank Heavy Press,* and *Carnival.*

In addition to his writing, Thomas is the publisher of Arroyo Seco Press. One of the goals of Arroyo Seco Press is to publish poets who do not yet have a collection published. His website is: thomasrthomas.org.

Also by Los Nietos Press

Dancing in the Santa Ana Winds: Poems y Cuentos New and Selected, liz gonzález (2018)

California Trees, Kit Courter (2018)

Wingless, Linda Singer (2017)

Sharing Stories: Global Voices Coming Together, Various Authors (2016)

The Beatle Bump, Clifton Snider (2016)

Yearlings, Frank Kearns (2015)

So Cali, Trista Dominqu (2015)

Persons of Interest, Lorine Parks (2015)

ABOUT
LOS NIETOS PRESS

Los Nietos Press is dedicated to the countless generations of people whose lives and labor created the world community that today spreads over the coastal floodplain known simply as Los Angeles.

We take our name from the Los Nietos Spanish land grant that was south and east of the downtown area. Our purpose is to serve local writers so they may share their words with many, in the form of tangible books that can be held and read and passed on. This written art form is one way we realize our common bonds and help each other discover what is meaningful in life.

LOS NIETOS PRESS
www.LosNietosPress.com
LosNietosPress@Gmail.com

www.ingramcontent.com/pod-product-compliance
Lightning Source LLC
Chambersburg PA
CBHW072041040426
42447CB00012BB/2970